HEY GOD, I'M HAVING AN AWFUL VACATION IN EGYPT THANKS TO MOSES!

W9-DDK-518

THE FROG TELLS
HER SIDE OF
THE STORY

TROY SCHMIDT
ILLUSTRATED BY CORY JONES

SO I GOT THIS VACATION BROCHURE AND HEARD THAT THE NILE RIVER WAS BEAUTIFUL THIS TIME OF YEAR. BUT, AS I JUMPED OFF THE BOAT, I SAW THE MOST DISGUSTING THING. THE NILE WAS GLOPPY AND RED. THIS WAS NOT RIGHT! THE BROCHURE SHOWED THE NILE AS BEAUTIFUL AND BLUE.
I DECIDED TO COMPLAIN. A LITTLE, BITTY GNAT TOLD ME THAT SOME GUY NAMED PHARAOH WAS IN CHARGE OF THIS AREA. I HEADED TO THE PALACE TO GIVE HIM A PIECE OF MY MIND.

WHEN I ARRIVED, PHARAOH WASN'T IN A GOOD MOOD EITHER. STANDING BEFORE HIM WAS SOME OLD GUY WEARING STINKY, DIRTY CLOTHES, WHO LOOKED LIKE HE HAD BEEN HANGING OUT WITH SHEEP ALL DAY. "MOSES, TURN THE NILE BLUE AGAIN!" PHARAOH DEMANDED. "LET MY PEOPLE GO," MOSES SHOT BACK. SO THIS WAS THE GUY WHO RUINED MY VACATION. MOSES. HE'S THE ONE WHO TURNED THE NILE RED. I NEEDED TO TALK TO HIM—FACE TO FACE.

I HOPPED UP ON MOSES' CLOAK. BUT BEFORE THE FIRST WORD CAME TO THE TIP OF MY RATHER LONG TONGUE, MOSES HELD ME UP TO HIS FACE. "HELLO, FROG," HE SAID.

"GOD HAS SHOWED ME THAT YOU'RE ABOUT TO GET SOME COMPANY."

WHAT?! I THOUGHT. COMPANY! I CAME HERE TO GET AWAY FROM EVERYONE! BUT BEFORE I COULD SAY A WORD, MOSES LIFTED HIS STAFF AND THEN . . .

IT COULD. ONCE THE FROGS WERE GONE, BILLIONS OF NASTY GNATS FLEW INTO TOWN. I USUALLY DON'T MIND HAVING A GNAT OR TWO AROUND. BUT THEY WERE ALL OVER THE PEOPLE, ALL OVER THE COWS—THEY WERE EVERYWHERE! THIS WAS JUST TOO MUCH. I FOUND THAT GNAT I SPOKE TO BEFORE. HE WASN'T TOO HAPPY EITHER. ALL OF HIS RELATIVES FLEW INTO TOWN, AND HE DIDN'T HAVE ENOUGH FOOD TO FEED THEM ALL! NOW I WAS REALLY GETTING MAD, HOPPING MAD!

BUT MY TERRIBLE VACATION DIDN'T END THERE. AFTER THE GNATS LEFT, BUZZING FLIES MOVED IN. NOW I LIKE FLIES. THEY ARE A FROG'S FAVORITE FOOD. BUT BOY ARE THEY NOISY! IMAGINE MILLIONS OF BUZZES ALL BUZZING AT THE SAME TIME. IT WAS SO NOISY, I EVEN LOST MY APPETITE. PHARAOH'S HEART GOT MAD. AND I GOT MADDER.

THEN, EVERY MAN AND ANIMAL BROKE OUT IN SORES.
BIG, PUFFY, RED BUMPS APPEARED ON EVERYTHING—EVEN ME!
THEY WERE WORSE THAN WARTS!
PHARAOH'S HEART GOT MAD. AND I GOT MADDER.

I THOUGHT NOTHING COULD BE AS BAD AS THOSE NASTY SORES . . .
UNTIL THE HAIL CAME. GIANT BALLS OF ICE FELL FROM THE SKY,
CRASHING INTO THE GROUND, SMASHING EVERYTHING IN ITS PATH.
PHARAOH'S HEART GOT MAD. AND I GOT MADDER.

THEN CAME THE LOCUSTS.

LOCUSTS DEVOUR EVERYTHING IN SIGHT, AND THEY HAVE THE WORST TABLE MANNERS. THEY EAT WITH ALL SIX OF THEIR HANDS AND TALK WITH THEIR MOUTHS FULL. THEY DON'T EVEN USE A NAPKIN! SO NOW, I WAS OFFICIALLY ON THE WORST VACATION EVER WITH THE RUDEST INSECTS ON THE PLANET. CONGRATULATIONS TO ME! PHARAOH'S HEART GOT MAD, AND I GOT MADDER.

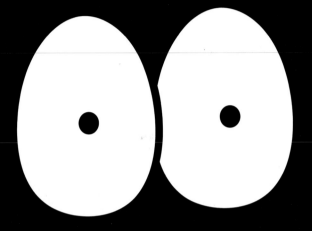

WHEN THE LOCUSTS LEFT, THEN CAME DARKNESS.
SOMEBODY TURNED OFF THE SUN! IT WAS SO DARK THAT I
COULDN'T SEE MY TONGUE IN FRONT OF MY FACE. I COULDN'T
MOVE BECAUSE I WAS AFRAID TO TRIP OVER SOMETHING.
SO I STOOD IN ONE PLACE—FOR DAYS.
PHARAOH'S HEART GOT MAD. AND I . . . DIDN'T GET MADDER.
I GOT SCARED. SO I TALKED TO GOD.

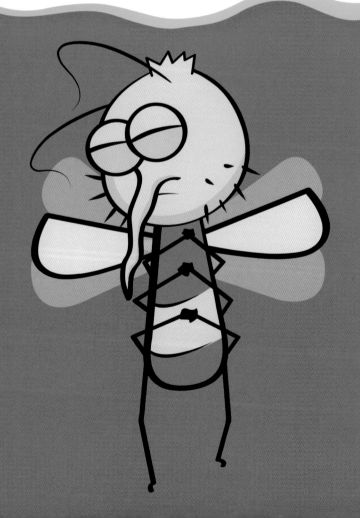

"GOD, I'M SORRY THAT I'VE BEEN SO SELFISH.
THIS VACATION HAS BEEN AWFUL, BUT INSTEAD OF GETTING MAD,
I SHOULD HAVE ASKED YOU FOR HELP AND STRENGTH."
GOD WAS NICE ABOUT IT. "THAT'S OKAY, FROG. I FORGIVE
YOU. YOU SEE, PHARAOH IS BEING SELFISH TOO. INSTEAD OF
LETTING MY PEOPLE GO, HE KEEPS DEMANDING THEY STAY AND
HELP HIM. NOW I MUST SHOW HIM HOW POWERFUL I AM.
IT'S THE WORST THING HE WILL EVER FACE. HURRY, I'LL
SHOW YOU WHERE TO GO SO THAT YOU'LL BE SAFE."

SO I HOPPED THE WAY GOD SHOWED ME, ALL THE WAY TO THE HOUSE OF AN ISRAELITE FAMILY. THEY WERE PREPARING THE HOUSE AND SHUTTING THE DOOR WHEN I SQUEEZED IN AT THE LAST MINUTE. INSIDE, THE FAMILY ATE A SPECIAL MEAL AS A TERRIBLE CRY ECHOED THROUGH THE STREETS. I DIDN'T WANT TO KNOW WHAT WAS HAPPENING, BUT I KNEW I WAS SAFE.